Vicky is a retired educator, former English teacher, assistant principal and principal. She received her Ph.D. from Emory University in Educational Leadership with a concentration in English. She has been a lover of poetry and literature since she was very young. Vicky started writing poetry when she was in junior high school. It was then that she began to realize that she is a lesbian. She did not understand at the time that she is still a child of God. She has decided that she has something to say and wants to add her voice to the voices of the universe.

To Judy Dennison, my life's partner and inspiration.

To Nancy my mother who gave me my first book of poetry.

Ordering Information
Quantity sales: Special discounts are available on quantity purchases by corporations, associations, and others. For details, contact the publisher at the address below.

Publisher's Cataloging-in-Publication data
Ferguson, Vicky
Journeys

ISBN 9781638291923 (Paperback)
ISBN 9781638291930 (ePub e-book)

Library of Congress Control Number: 2023908557

www.austinmacauley.com/us

First Published 2023
Austin Macauley Publishers LLC
40 Wall Street, 33rd Floor, Suite 3302
New York, NY 10005
USA

mail-usa@austinmacauley.com
+1 (646) 5125767

Vicky Ferguson

JOURNEYS

AUSTIN MACAULEY PUBLISHERS™

LONDON • CAMBRIDGE • NEW YORK • SHARJAH

To Randy Fair, my friend who encouraged me to send my poetry into the world.

Table of Contents

The Poet Gives the Poem

God rhythmically
Chants
Through the pitter
    Patter
        Of raindrops
As the artist and the poet spew forth emotions
Pen and brush on canvases yellowed
By time and the passing of youthful dreams.

The artist's hands conduct a symphony of colors
Long, silent fingers
    Splash
        The hues of emotions
           Beliefs and hopes
Upon the yellow canvas of her soul.

The poet, too, paints a picture
Her hands conduct a symphony of sounds
All muted
    Falling
        On stone deaf ears.
The artist and poet sharing senses

Able to feel more deeply,
To see more clearly
Than the masses of stone-faced men
Who turn their eyes
    Inward upon stone hearts
        Devoid of humanity.

The artist's yellow canvas sings a song of life
Her colors strike chords in her heart and soul
    Her gifts too intense
        For the stone men to see
Their eyes blinded by shallowness
Her canvas
    Sings only
        To itself.

The Poet's yellow paper sings
Words cascade over each other
    And crescendo in the Poet's ears
        Who alone hears the message.

The Artist and the Poet
Bear gifts enough to save mankind
    From its tragic destiny,
        Devoid of beauty and love
The stone men, blind and deaf
Live in the valley of dry bones.

They draw inward in silence
And the Artist and the Poet
Sit smiling silently
Searching for someone to grasp
        Their gifts.

Journey to Self

Steps of My Childhood

Home
Or what used to be home
Now no more than three steps
Leading nowhere.

Road builders tore down the house
Leaving only worn out cement steps
And a cement patio
Covered now by nature's debris.

How ironic
To sit on the steps of my childhood
And yearn for the past
As I once sat and dreamed of the future.
Dreamed of being twenty
Who am now thirty
And know what it was like.

Dogwood in full bloom
Reminiscent of childhood
The stinkweed tree exudes the smell
Pervading my girlhood.

The grass unkempt and knee high
Still invites me to shed shoes
And become a kid again.

Three steps
Countless hours of childhood spent
Emotions of my being ingrained in the cement
Tears after my first bicycle wreck
Bathed these steps.

Eternities spent on the patio
Cool summer evenings
Sweltering summer nights
Shrouded in the smell of the stinkweed tree
A family sat and talked of everything and nothing.

Three steps
        Soon to be bulldozed
To be covered by progress
The dogwood bloom to be a memory
Land leveled and graded
        Covered by asphalt.

My childhood lost to freeways
And fast-moving vehicles
No more will I sit on these three steps
I who was three and am now thirty
Am the house of my childhood.

The Last Dance

Music screaming
And tap, tap, tapping no more
Numbness from feet spreading upward.

Music
Crescendo
Destroying
Like a bomb
         f
         a
         l
         l
         i
         n
         g
On innocent children.

Can't dance anymore—
Not now, my heart laid open
Pig-like, waiting dissection.

Mad whirling dance
        STOPPED!
Stillness
Like a church at night
And shadows out of darkness bright
Tap, tap, tapping
Lift me, whirl me 'round
Keep me twirling.

But the beat is gone
And the shadow drawn
        Cannot force my feet
                To keep tap, tap, tapping.

Letting Go

Emptying myself out
In the moonlight outside my window
Peeping through bare branches of trees
The glow of the moon
Like a magnet
Pulls the tide of deep grief buried
In years of pseudo intellect
Soul wails
          At the prospect
                    Of emptiness
                              And vulnerability.

Emptying myself out in the moonlight
Like a volcano
Lies spew forth leaving me limp
Rag doll-like
          Bent from waist
                    Fingers reaching for the floor
                              To break the fall.
Empty…
Moonlight
Warm glow

And at the core is a cross
        Suffering servant
                Hanging, bloodied
                        And beautiful
Silence
        Peace
                Hope
Life.

Discovering Ghost Ranch

Closing my eyes
I feel the power of this place
　　　　Native American spirits whirl around me
I open myself to the silence of the mountains
And hear a peaceful humming
　　　　Inviting and comforting
A tree shades me
And I feel its presence
Welcoming me to this place.

Eyes wide open to beautiful trees
Bursting with color
Forming a blanket of yellow
Against the red hills
Backing up to the deep blue mountains
Come quietly to me
Then I can ingest your beauty.

O Mother Earth
　　　　Travel through my feet that guide my journey
Fill me with your energy
　　　　And lead me to wisdom

Majestic Mountains
       Send your spirit down to me
Fill me with your majesty and silence
       So I can hear the voices of my ancestors
Emerging from the stillness.

Father Sky
       Brilliantly blue with wispy, white clouds
Covering the earth
       Cover me with your spirit
Sister Sun
       Send your rays of heat
To warm my disconnected soul
       Light my way along my journey
Until Brother Moon
       Rises in the sky
Blessed bright light to the darkness
       Keep me from stumbling along my journey
Earth, Mountain, Trees, Sky, Sun, Moon
       Merge your spirits into one
And awaken my soul.

Hearing My Voice

I hear it
Coming from somewhere
Deep inside me
Always there
Nagging me to listen long enough
To hear the lesson
And still I flee
Afraid of what will be said
Afraid to unpack my life
Full of secrets
Dark and drear
Packed away
In lidded boxes
Ordered
Controlled
Safe
And I
Afraid to step out of the shadow
To beg the question
Afraid
Of answer reverberating
In my brain

Of my life
Deemed unnatural
Stuffed in boxes
Neatly packed
Away from my reality
Still the ghost haunts me
Beckons me
To feel its embrace
To hear its breath
Coming in short
Excited gasps
To make love
Passionate
Unrelenting
Sweet.
And the aftermath
Of passion
Is the whisper
"Come closer
Hear your voice
Clarion clear
Full of poetry."

Stranger

Stranger
Gone too long
I wanted to search for you
Instead I fled into the darkness
Of my soul and packed up
Pain and misery
As if by packing it up
I could shove it into a dark corner.

I've watched you though
Watched from afar
Dreaming of being you
Who knows
My life
Too afraid to beckon you
Invite you
To journey with me.

Left you in the wilderness
To perish in the desert
While I kept
My misery packed up

In Pandora-like boxes
Still you followed me
Listening to the deafening silence
When you wanted camaraderie
I was too afraid
To ask questions
That might unravel my universe
Throwing me off the wall
Like Humpty Dumpty
And leaving me scattered
Across the floor
In a million pieces.

Stranger
Because I refused
To force you
From imagination to reality
You remained
In the wilderness
Alone and frightened
Until I
At last let my soul scream
Until syllables
Garbled at first
Become louder and louder
Voice resonating
With richness
      And music
          And truth
Voice compelled to sing

Or die

And now you are here

Friend

Companion

Writer.

The Second Singing of the Birds

Life spent
Awakening
To the first singing of birds
My soul
A sun
Slow-rising
Then suspended
Between dark and light.

Hanging
Purgatory-like
Waiting for clouds to subside
Before stepping out
Into its own shadow
Waiting
For God to let go his brush.

Waiting
For the sun to shine through
Like a ball of fire
Splashing red paint
On the horizon
Waiting to hear
The second singing of the birds.

Waiting

Naked trees
Winter bare outside my window
Reaching out
      Their empty arms
            Pulling me into woods
                Dark and deep
Showing me secrets nature hides
      Deer trampling dead leaves
            Long since lost their colors
Nakedness
      Exposing imperfections
            Knotted and gnarled, stooped and bent
Broken
Yet exuding a certain pride
Struggling to stand tall
      To spread arms towards heaven
            And wait for spring.

Fish out of Water

Two wooden fish
Hand painted
　　　Swimming on my windowsill
Red, green, orange, blue
Flowers for gills
　　　Mouth poised to steal bait
Or take the hook
Big eyes
　　　A butterfly appears to fly between
Fish out of water.

Some days I am
Those wooden fish
　　　Brightly colored
　　　　　Sans gills for breathing
Suffocating
　　　Missing the bait
　　　　　Swallowing the hook
Until squinting my eyes
　　　Green trees on other side of window
　　　　　Become a green ocean
Washing me into the surf.

Closet Dwellers

Once upon a time in the not so distant past
In a land not so far away,
There lived closet dwellers…

I

Closets are dark dwellings
Fit for clothes, hanging
Color coded in neat rows
For shoes stuffed in boxes
With secrets tucked inside
Not made for human beings
To take refuge there
Hiding
Deep in dark recesses
Closet dwellers
Like frightened cave dwellers
Hide from the light
And scribble secrets on the walls.

II

We became closet dwellers
As soon as we knew
Adolescent girls
Yearn to glimpse the jungle
Offering pleasure
To feel the gushing wet
Fluid on their fingers
And tongues
Macho boys
Slyly gaze at the bulge
Hugged by too-tight jeans
Wanting only to touch
To feel the hardness
To suck the sweet love.

III

Why can't we come out?
       Come out and play?
Come out
And play like other children
Red rover, red rover
Send queers right over
London Bridge is falling down
Falling down
       Falling down
And we stay locked up inside ourselves
Living a dual life

Wearing two masks
　　　　One for them
Disguising our queerness.
And
One for us
Hiding from ourselves
Years later, we dare to remember.

IV

Therapy, we went seeking salvation
From strangers
Who didn't know us or love us
Therapists, our closet angels
Closet dust choking us
Until we kiss the sleeping princess inside
Until we throw off the mantle of fear and be
Angels bright, make us know we are all right.

V

Closet dwellers, nocturnal bats
Sun goes down
Fly out, head to town
Breathe life into pictures
Drawn on closet walls
Huddled in smoky masses
Hiding fears
Of exposure and HIV
In alcohol and poppers

The ringmaster yells out, "Play the play!"
Leather-clad men become macho
Waiting to grope Mr. Right
And dykes acting like men to attract women
And the beat goes on
     As madness whirls
          Around and around
Until the music comes to a screeching halt
Afraid of dawn, closet dwellers
Flee home in pairs, knowing
That tomorrow the prince
Won't come bearing a glass slipper
So they change masks
And go into the lonely world.

Lesbos and Fags come out at night
Lesbos and Fags come out at night
Lesbos and Fags come out at night
To dance and sing
Incognito.

VI

Dykes
Young girls hiding their tender souls
In boys' clothes and tough swaggers
Young girls hold on
Don't go gently into manhood
Hold on
Don't let them rob you of the fruit

Between your athletic legs
And your supple breasts
Ripe for the picking.
Throw back your shoulders
Proud to be a lesbian
Kiss the sleeping princess
Within and awaken her.

Lesbos and Fags come out at night
Lesbos and Fags come out at night
Lesbos and Fags come out at night
To dance and sing
Incognito.

VII

Debutantes – rich and pretty girls
Sticking together, afraid to mingle
Or of becoming one of those people
Their caves uptown furnished
With all the right trappings
And like clothes they hang close
One to the other
Afraid for their jobs, their very lives
They hide dark and deep in closets
From the riffraff like drag queens
And bull dykes.
Closet dwelling debutantes
Too good for the gay world
Play society's game and

Pretend to wait for prince charming.

VIII

Joyful queen,
Masquerading
Your whole life as a woman
"Mirror, mirror on the wall,
Who is the prettiest queen of all?"
"Faggot, Faggot incognito"
But oh, the beauty
Of your soul
Hidden in closets
Dark and deep
Until night falls
And you sling your boa
Around slightly stooped shoulders
Strut your stuff
Ready to dance and sing
In the twirling lights
Of the disco
You go, girl!

Lesbos and Fags come out at night
Lesbos and Fags come out at night
Lesbos and Fags come out at night
To dance and sing
Incognito.

IX

Oh, James Dean
How I longed to be you
Sulking
Rebellious
Gooood looking
Blond hair swooped
Off your troubled brow
With a fuck the World
Smirk
You knew
Even then—young as you were
You knew you had to be
Fuck the rest of the world
You lived fast and hard
And died too young
You knew to turn
Your collar to the wind
And be
Some thirty years later
You're dead and I am
For the first time
In my life
I AM
Turning my collar
To the wind
I AM!

Lesbos and Fags, come out
Lesbos and Fags, come out
Lesbos and Fags, come out
Come sing and dance
Come sing and dance
In
The
Broad
Daylight.

X

Coming out
Coming out of closets dark
Coming out
Not 18 or dressed in white
Of vestal virgins;
No vestiges
Of virginity
No debutante ball
Closeted since 12
Covered with closet dust
I thought myself ugly
Until at 51
Teenage snapshots
Look back at me
Reflecting beauty
No deformity
Mirrored on the outside
Coming out

Revising secrets
Scribbled on closet walls
Facing a world
Full of bigotry and hate
Defended with God's word
Coming out of the closet
Risking all that I am
And yet
The closet is too deadly dark
Throw open the doors
Here I am
Come out
To see the world
Come out proud
Unafraid
Into the light of day
A debutante at last
Presented to the world
A child of God
Strike up the band
     Take my hand
          And twirl around the floor
          In jubilation!

New Life

Listen
Be very quiet and listen
And somewhere far, far away, echo the sounds of days
gone by
It is fall again and crickets and the cool night air
Beckon the end of another summer
And awakens me to the possibility of rebirth
Rebirth, a strange word to consider
At the onslaught of dying leaves
But even so the end of summer
Dresses itself in blazing colors
That mystify the soul.

Fall
Not from grace but from deadened illusions
That I once chased like a mad hound
Trying to tree a fox
Illusions shattered by the burst of radiance
That is fall.

Now I know the answer
Lies within my being
And that of two small children
And their mother
Windows and refrigerators
Covered with children's artwork
And little boy's clothes strewn on bathroom floors.
Boxes of life stuffed and stacked in every corner
Ready to be sorted and cast away
Left empty like the trees of leaves.

Awakening to the middle years
And baseball and ballet
And dogs and cats and hamsters
Discoveries of life here for exploration.

And you woman
Like me and different
In the way you try to tree the fox.

Let us take this new fall as a beginning
A rebirth
Kicking, sliding out of the womb.
Let we two women
Put away the pain and hurt
And see each other
        A bit tarnished with age
            To give way
                To new life in the spring.

Sanity and Where You Find It

Welcome to my sanity
Not long ago we sat and composed a poem of sorts
To welcome visitors to your condo on St. Simons
Condo that is no more

Still sanity and beaches
Ring echoes in our lives of the day to day
Don't you think it's about time
To bottle beach sanity and let it escape
Like sand from an hourglass
Into our lives
     Away from beach
         And dunes
             And sea oats?

You are my sanity
And insanity and lover
And companion and soul mate
Wherever we plant our feet
In sand or on concrete.

Come live with me and be my love
And we will romp through sandcastles and sand dunes
Through daffodils and tulips
Through the concrete jungles of our lives
And we will stop and unleash our sanity
Unafraid, unabashedly.

On one knee
Will you marry me?
Join your sanity and insanity with mine?
Forgetting the pain, the suffering of sanity past
And harnessing our purity of heart
Till death do us part
And even into eternity?

God
Give me the wisdom
        The patience
                And the peace
To love and cherish
This fleeting moment in eternity.

The Atlantic

I have come home again
To the Atlantic Ocean
The ocean
I know best
The mighty ocean that roars
As its waves hit the shore
My ocean
The one full of memories.

Ocean roar
Pierce my soul
Blow your breeze onto my face
Lick my feet
As I walk your shore
Ease the world from me
If for just a few hours
Still my racing brain
Fill me with a peace
Only offered by your roar.

Paradise Found

Welcome to our sanity
Little house aglow
With soft yellow
Rays of sunlight.

Welcome to our sanity
A sleepy Venice town
Sans
Traffic jams
Ringing phones
Rushing places
Resting peace.

Welcome to our sanity
Where no one
Expects us
To solve their problems
Have the answers
Make it all run smoothly.

Welcome to our sanity
Sans spaces
Too full
To breathe.

Welcome
Catch the ferry
Walk the beach
Breathe
Hunt sharks' teeth
Welcome
To our paradise.

New Ocean

And now a new ocean
Different from the one
Of my youth
This ocean of my maturity
Is more suited
To who I am now
Calming
Embracing me
Instead of giving me
Tumultuous rides
On its breaking waves.

Blue green in color
Clear enough
To see my feet
This new ocean
Sings soft songs.

The gulf may be more suitable
But the Atlanta still beckons me
To times long gone
When we walked
Together with blue herons
Relishing the sea breeze
On our faces
And sea foam on our feet.

Young and welcoming
The fierceness of the ocean
We rode the waves
You and I
Gleefully
And now we enter cautiously
Into the calm gulf
Holding hands
To keep our footing
In the shifting sands
Of time.

Journey to Parenthood

For Anne

I love you
I know
I didn't have
To ache in childbirth
I didn't get to help
Name you
But you're mine anyway.
The way you walk
And talk is me
The way you look
And your kindness
Is your mom
And your temperament
Is both of us
Oh, we know
We're different
And that's hard
For you to understand
But you will someday.
You will know
That it's okay
That we're

The best friends
For a little girl
Who is a mixture
Of the finest
In us both.

I love you
Sunshine
And
Rain
It will always be the same.

Dark Times I

A young girl
Cries for her daddy
Turned bitter
By his own hatred
For her mother
Hatred
Dripping
Like fresh blood
Puddling
Around his heart
Until his emotions
Drown
And his daughter's
Heart breaks.

Dark Times II

Dark times tried to smother your soul
Suck it from you
Leaving you
Dry and brittle
      Desolate
But
You found the ball of fire
And the sun
Broke up the clouds
And you
Claimed your life
Took back your soul
And came home
The prodigal daughter
In the sunlight.

Poetry Read

Kissing frogs is easy
When the eleven-year-old girl
Who generally wants to drive you crazy
Wants tonight to read poetry
In the middle
Of the living room floor
Amid
      Chips, hot chocolate
           Wine
And memories
What special memories
We build tonight
Kissing frogs
On the living room floor
Kissing frogs
And turning into princesses.

Leaving Home

My son left today
To go be a man
An awesome task
For a 12-year-old
Needed his real father
A lesbian.
Couldn't fill the void.
I've loved John though
For some six years
Hoped I could ease the pain
Of him missing his dad
I couldn't.
I miss him with my soul
And I hope against all hope
That I gave him something to grow on
Some semblance of humanity
And kindness
And love.

Wish I had a little boy
And his name were John
He would be
The sweetest little boy
In the whole wide world.

Maybe I do
Maybe I do.

For John

Wish I had a little boy
And his name were John
He would be the sweetest
Little boy in the whole wide world
You were 12 and I was 48
And you were the son I never had
I wanted to be a good parent
And you wanted to be loved
You, a victim of the war of roses
Waged between parents' pain
You needed your father and I needed you.

Then pain captured your easy emotions
Your eyes glazed and you lost the wonderment
Of the little boy flying a kite over ocean blue
Shell shocked you fled love's grasp
I miss you with my soul and hope against hope
That I gave you something to grow on
Some semblance of humanity and kindness and love.

Wish I had a little boy
And his name were John
He would be the sweetest
Little boy in the whole wide world.

Now you are 21 and I am 57
We see you on holidays
Never long enough
Your mother is gracious
I, bitter and begrudging
Forgiveness haunts me.

And you were 12 and I was 48
I was stupid to think
          You could fight the dragon
Without coming home
          On your shield.
Instead I come
          My body bloodied
                    My shield laid down
Begging your forgiveness
To throw open my prison door
And set me free.

Escaping the Dragon

I was 12
You were 48
And somehow
We
Got lost
      In a time-warp
No resurrection.

Now 21
Yearning
      To tell tales
Of sorrow
Despair
To free us both.

Instead I cry
Unable to ask
      Your forgiveness
And come home.

We were ageless
And innocent
Pain pulsating
Hardened hearts
      Frightened us
We huddled
In dark corners
      Counting
Our thirty pieces
Of silver.

All who have ears
To hear
      Listen to the pain
All who have eyes
To see
Watch love
      Steal us both
           From the Dragon's teeth.

Dance of the Dolphins

The dolphins danced for us
On that glorious February day
Nature's own symphony
Beckoned us on that trip to Savannah
Great blues greeted us from the salt marshes
Good luck omens we thought
You, the girl and I headed to Tybee
For a respite from court fears.

Had nature sent only blue herons
We would have been thankful
But it was as if nature herself
Played a symphony just for us
The great blues, the first movement
Then the gulls and sand dollars
Climaxing in the dolphin ballet
Eight of them in graceful movement
Along the coastline.

A perfect day
Just you, the girl and me
Walking on the beach
Reveling in nature's symphony.

A Blue Plastic Glass

A plain blue plastic glass…
Images of you drinking death's nectar…
Haunting.
A glass…a weapon…
Your mouth welcoming
The cold, smooth barrel
Hesitantly at first
Then completely
Sucking the barrel as it fired
Pill after pill into your stomach.

The horror of the deed
You lie on the cold
Hard bathroom floor
Alongside the blue plastic glass
Fallen.

Closed eyes see girls
Knee deep
In rumpled bathroom
Heads thrown back
Hands holding blue plastic glasses
Half full of sorrow
Half empty of life
Two of you reached stalemate
No more bargaining.
You stand eyeball to eyeball
Drinking death.

Closed eyes see you standing there
Staring at each other
Through red lipstick messages
Scrawled by hands
Gripping blue glasses
Until lives explode
Shattering.

Closed eyes see you there
Disappearing into the mirror
Hauntingly
Image after image play
And replay in my brain
Heads thrown back in triumph
Sipping death
From blue plastic glasses.

And now you're back
Mirror squeaky clean
Room squeaky clean
Your soul mud-caked
From the rains,
Still the image haunts me
Knots in stomach
A reminder that all is not perfect
As self-inflicted scars
On your arms and wrist
Remind you of
Dreams snatched
From your hands by razor sharp
Life almost cut short
Saved by your alarm
Screaming loud enough at midnight
To wake the dead.

Gut led, your mother,
Trusting you and God
Got in bed with you
Kept you from disappearing
Into the mirror…
You snuggled up to her spoon style
Your rump in her stomach.

As if you needed to back up
Into the protection of her womb
To die in the arms
Of she who birthed you
She yanked you from death's hand
Saved you from yourself
Gave birth the second time
As her screams for help
Pierced the silent night
Screams of labor resounding
Off walls until help arrived
Carted you off.

And I was left staring at a blue plastic glass
Knowing I had witnessed you sucking on the barrel.

Dancing into the Light

Come
Pull the fish from the pain
Raw, wrenching, retched pills, paralyzing
Shattered glass
Mirror reflecting message scribbled in red lipstick
"I AM NOT HERE!"

Bleeding wrists and death
Dancing seductively
Fancy stepping, sliding cross your life
Beckoning you to join the dance.

Twirl away
Twirl away.

Come

Pull the fish from the pain

Madness dressed in many colored skirt

Whirls around you, color bleeding into color

Dancing at a fevered pitch

Enveloping you with promises of peace

Twirl away

Twirl away

Come

Pull the fish from the pain

Ashen, you lay at stairs top

Lifeless

Slipping away, smack of hand slapping

Docile face.

Sounds of life resounding

Breaking deafening silence

Life

      Grabs your hand

And

      Dances you into the light.

Arizona

An Arizona
Grand Canyon
    Deep enough
        To fill with dreams
        Of futures.
Sedona
    Beautiful enough
        To lead you
        To your spirit.

An Arizona
Desert
Rich and hot
    To remind you
    That God is great.

Mountains
Majestic and still
    To lure you
    With their secrets.

Native Americans
      Proud and hungry
      To share their spirits
      With the hungry soul.

Yes, Anne
There is an Arizona
      A place of refuge
      When the night is too dark
            When the day is too stark
                  And the shadows surround you
Remember somewhere
There is an Arizona.

Journey to God

What Must I Do or Be or Think or Feel?

What do I find on the interior
      When I crawl down
            Deep inside my being?

What aromas do I smell?
What flavors do I taste?
What images do I see?
What melodies do I hear?
What surfaces do I touch?

Am I living by default?
      Do I ride the waves
            But try to control the tide?
What's deep down
      In the recesses
            Of my being?

A little girl holding armless hand?

Frightened and alone
Eyes wild and darting
Emotions raw
Tangled up inside
Twisted heart
Crying out in pain
Thirsting for water
To sooth parched mouth and swollen tongue.

Drums of abandonment.

And I step into the waters
Wading deeper
And deeper
Until the water hugs my neck
And tries creeping over my head
Washing me clean.

And it is truth driving me
        And forcing me
                Day after day
To pound the keyboard
Truth appearing on the screen.

And so, it is that I must write
Or my soul will dry up and blow
In the winds
My angst is torn from me
Starving my need to form words
To make sense
So I can listen
To my life's rhythms
Searching for space
To create and play and laugh and cry
Space to empty myself out into the universe
　　　Refill myself with words and images
Life space to wait upon the voice of God.

Labyrinth

It was a small room
Floor turned into labyrinth
Room, a retreat into silence
Sisters walking journey
With me and apart from me
Slowly moving to the center
Stopping to pray along the way
       Stopping often
              Mumbling words
                    Flowing from the soul
Beautiful petitions for answers
Finally whispering
Bless me
Give me the blessing God
       Crying out
              For the blessing
                    Trembling
                        Frightening
Silence slowly trumpeting in my ears
Voice rising
       Coming from deep inside my soul
You are blessed

I bless you
You have always had my blessing
      And the light shone
           In the center
                  Of my mind's eye
And I wept in thankfulness.

Sacred Moment

She sits still
Listens
Sounds of silence
Slip into whispers
She hears
And feels the wind
Ever so gently
On her face
Energizing.

Soul dry as the valley
Of bones
Burning bush
And who shall I say sent me?
Tell them it is the wind
Blowing through the room
And through your soul
That helps you find words
To praise and cry and love and die.

Wind and words and wonderment
Fight for her soul
Leading
Her into desert dry
Striking stones
Spewing
Bubbling baptismal waters.

Tell them it is the wind
Blowing
Through the room
And your soul
Helping you find words
To praise and cry and love and die.

Opening herself
To the flow
Of joy
Trusting wind dancing
Around her
Bringing peace
And a sacred moment.

From the Gut

From the gut
A well soul deep spews clear, cool water
Washing over my sorrow
Releasing pain into the cosmos
It comes from the gut
The awe at the indescribable beauty
Offered up by nature herself
Holding the sunrise and the sunset in her hands.
Like a magician.

The woods dark and deep
Beckon the traveler to find solace
In a world gone gut wrenching mad.

And Jesus, sweet Jesus calls us to stand
In his footsteps
To eat at his table
To drink his blood
And still we don't get it.
Like the twelve who stumbled,
We cannot hear his voice in the wind.
We pray and prance around in his presence
But we hear not.

Like stone men, our ears are closed
        Our tongues are dry
                Our eyes are blind.

And where do we begin to find answers?
In the river?
Dare we step out of the boat onto the water?

"Turn and listen to my voice in your soul
        Listen to the rolling water
                Offer promises of cleansing and renewal
Feel the light and the beauty
        Of unspeakable emotion
                Roll over you."

Voice grabs me
From the everyday circus of our lives
And bids me pay attention.

Fisher of Men

We came
Looking for God
From the ash heaps
Lost in the hatefulness
    Of child custody battles
We came to the ocean
Hoping to hear God's voice
    In the ocean's roar
Hoping to see his majesty
    Personified in seagulls' flight
Pelicans' salute
A sign
Like Israelites lost in the wilderness
Faith failing
    We needed a sign.

Never in dreams wild
Did we dare to hope?
For the Fisher of Men Himself
Waiting for us on the beach before daybreak
Waiting to walk with us
          Bringing balm
                    For our weary souls.

First the white heron
Pure and silent
Met us
Then each new morn before daybreak
          Two great blues
                    Waiting for us
A sign
As if He torched the sea oats
          One greeted us
                    Then the other
Both in turn waited
Along the beach
          Great blues
                    Tall
          Majestic
                    Peaceful
Waiting to walk us
Back into memories
Of a time
When our faith was stronger
That God would bring us
Out of the wilderness.

And now we know
Standing eyeball to eyeball
With the Fisher of Men
Whose wingspan is great enough
To carry us
Now we know
It is He
The Fisher of Men
Disguised and unmasked simultaneously
Standing before us
Beckoning us onward
      Taking flight
           And then stopping somewhere
Waiting for us
      Waiting to feed
           Our hungry souls.

Salvation

Soul parched
Valley of dry bones
Wind
Blowing
Click, click
Clicking of camera
      Capturing little girl
            Tongue swollen thick
Voiceless
Trembling
In glow of burning bush.

Click
Click
Little girl tapping stone
      Baptismal waters
Listening
      To the wind
            And feeling
God's breath
      On her face.

Unnamable

Valley of dry bones
And Yahweh said
"I am that I am."

Yet we cry out
In the wilderness
"We are what we are."

Bones
Bunched together
Company to walk roads
To the garden
Uneven roots, boots trample
Narcissus.

Forsythia
Arms reaching
To the sun
And we raise
Our arms
Searching
For the son
Of man
Who cries
"I am that I am."

Sweet smelling narcissus.

And we try to echo
"I am…"

Narcissus filled nostrils
Self-rooted in stuffed words.

Parched throats
Silent cries
And Yahweh cries
"I am that I am!"

We answer
In unison
"I am that I am
Is not enough!"

Not yet
For we are what we are
Huddled together
Shivering
In the cold
Darkness
Sweating
In the heat
Of the ash heap.

And Yahweh cries out,
"I am that I am."

"Listen
        Be still
                Hear your life's
                        Melody
                                Full of cacophonies
Still
It is your garden
Music.

Follow
The music
Leading to the edge
Of the garden
As it pipes its way
Into the woods
Dance naked
Among the trees."

Dance of dry bones.

"We are afraid
Our nakedness
Scares us
We want to stay
In the garden."

Bone to bone
Jangling
Stumbling
Over protruding
Roots.

"It is too late
Knowledge
Not nakedness
Lost you Eden."

God's music blares
I feel the wind kissing my cheek.

Holding hands with the trees
We dance
Sure-footed
With spirit
Wild!

Footsteps on My Shadow

Sweet Jesus
Like a stinger in my brain
Burning into my weary soul
You've dogged me
For years
Footsteps on my shadow
Stepping in time
To my stumbling
Laughing
At my foolishness
Crying
At my sorrow
     But always
          Embracing me.

Mesmerized
By your picture imprinted in my brain
Always moving forward
Coming closer
Whispering to me in the darkest night
Until I turned and saw you
That ragged figure
Who had pursued me for years
Moving ever closer.

Even when I loathed
Myself the most
You were there, loving me.

And now I get it
        I understand
                That I can only be
When I acknowledge
In my arrogance
That I AM
I AM a child of God.

Spiritually excommunicated
No more…

Journeys with Sister Women

Shirley

Sister woman
Soul sister
A poem for you
The keeper of my sanity
And laughter
And perspective
Who can always make me laugh
No matter what
How I have loved your spirit
And the essence that is you
Seems as if I have known you
All my life
A connection inexplicable
The binds us, one to the other
Different women we
You, straight and traditional
I, a lesbian

And yet we click
In all the right ways
I love you for who you are
And who I am
When we share the moments we do
Together and apart
Sister woman.

Beautiful Black Woman

Black woman, you're beautiful
With eyes of proud African queens
Too proud to look at the ground
And be held captive by white
Southern rednecks' riding herd
On rich man's slaves.

Black woman, you're beautiful
Full of voices echoing the past
Voices so vibrant, so soft
Voices of love caressing
White man's woes
Of plans gone wrong.

Black woman, you're beautiful
With hands of love comforting
Our weary souls, grown tired
Hands once bound by slavery's
Cankering chain cutting
Too deeply into womanly flesh.

Black woman, you're beautiful
Body too lovely to be used
For white man's lust
Too sacred to be raped
And brutally flesh-torn
By white man's bloody penetration.

Black woman, you're beautiful
With words of power, of love
Once muted by white ignorance
Now ringing out and piercing
The too long, too loud silence
Of suffering black women.

Truck Stop Mary

Truck stop Mary
Blond hair flying
Tight jeans hugging
Oversized buttocks
Uncovered
By loose black top.

Of all the faces
Only you
Have stayed with me
Eyes puffy
And outlined with crowfeet
Eyes
Piercing my soul.

Truck stop Mary
Slinging your smile
With hash browns on the side
Only your face
Has stayed
With me over the miles.
The blind traveler

Thinks you're only
A waitress
For he fails to see
Eyes that know
Steel gray and blue eyes
Singing a measure of joy
To a deaf and blind world.

Separate Flights

I watched the gulls today
Soaring
On the river front
And I remembered all the gulls
And oceans
And how we soared
Together
You and I.

Memories
Not cloaked in sadness
Not black and bitter
Or wrapped in hate
But memories sweet
That validate
Our present need
For separate flights.

Snapshots

Marilyn
Silenced
No sound escapes the gallery
Save the imaginary click
Of the camera making love to you
Click, click
Stopping time
Capturing you behind glass frames
Draped in white
Your body beckons me
Eyes wide open and alive
Pull me into your soul
Drowning in your sensuousness
Until the full stench
Of tragedy fills my nostrils
And like the click of the camera
My eyelids blink
Catapulting me into reality
And I weep for us both
Norma Jean.

Three Girls

In the midst of a noisy city
Three voices formed words
Of contentment and misery
Our voices fell silent
Under yours which cried
Misery trapped in a steel and glass world
The syllables became a bridge
Which linked our souls eternally.

Our paths crossed in a crowded city
And among the noise of life
We hung out together more or less
For four or five years
It is hard to keep track of love
And in the space of time, we grew
Together we loved, thought and fought
Over Emerson and philosophies of life.

Somehow, against the clamor of life
We all became a part of each other
In all the chaos of the city
Our souls touched each other
And sparked fleeting moments
Of beauty—now gone forever
And we should all be sad
And somehow we are not
For the friendship we shared
Has been much too important
To cry over.

On Your Departure

You've gone and you've taken
A part of me with you
And I don't like it
Part of me left as you drove away
And even though I know
That we will always be friends
I still don't like it.

You took part of the beauty
Out of my life—simply took it
And drove away
True you left
Part of your being here—but it's not
The same as it once was
And I don't like it.

I know that it's nobody's fault
I know people meet
Love each other and part every day
I know that nothing is forever
Not really, not even friendship
And I don't like it.

I also know that I was lucky
To have you—even for a short
Space of time
We may never
Have met, loved, laughed, cried
For the time we shared
I am eternally grateful.

I know you're gone
And nothing—not logic
Reason or anything else
Can make me like it
I still do not like it
I will never like it!

Delta Dawn Took a Great Fall

Delta Dawn is broken
She took a nosedive
Maybe she was tired
Of her faded rose
Or her place in life
Perched high above
Words of wisdom
Sequestered in the study
With me.

She didn't die though
With a pot of glue
She will be put back together again
The same way I did me
Sad, the pieces never seem to fit
Quite like they did before
Led by foolish fantasies
We try to fly too high.

I cried, kneeling
Over a broken mask
A tear ran down
My check
And landed on her faded rose
As it lay separated
From her suffering face.

I cried and thanked God
That we are not like
Humpty Dumpty.

Journey to Death

Ellen

Twelve years ago
Car wreck
DUI
Hospital exam
Lymphoma
A life-changing day.

Swollen spleen
Identified the spy
As indolent lymphoma
Hiding
Sneaking
Through your lymph nodes
Waiting
To spring to life
And invade your body.

And when you knew
He was watching you
You fled in fear
And denial
Not quick enough

Like a magic trick
He multiplied
Spread
Slowly
And then one day
He pulled off his mask
And stood boldly
Eyeball to eyeball
And pronounced
Your impending
Death sentence.

II

I sat
Lost in the sunset
Red sky
Bleeding
Into ocean blue
Seagulls
Flying overhead
I sat struck
By the beauty
Postcard perfect
Still
My thoughts
Wandered
Back to Roanoke
Small neighbor
Sans sunsets

And perfection
I, a silhouette
In the sunset
And you
My sister friend
Held captive
In your own body
By cancer cells
Sucking
Your sacred soul
Dry
And somewhere
In my sorrow
I wonder
What I did right
What you did wrong
Knowing
Deep inside
That the masked
Stranger
Like a force of fate
Stalks his victims
Indiscriminately.

III

It's treatment day
I call to inquire
About your treatment
To see if the poison

That eats
Your white blood cells
Had relaxed
So you can regenerate
Before they zap you
Once again
In attempts
To hunt down
The stranger
In your frail body
And kill him
Without killing you
The magic number
For your white count
Is three
Your count tops out
At 2.7
Time escapes
A thief in the night
Stealing your very life
You and the doc decide
To go for half a treatment
To inject
Your body
With more poison
To shrink the tumors
That grow
And crowd out
The other organs
In your abdominal cavity

…but
You're cheerful
When we talk
And hopeful.
I want
To ask
"Are you afraid?"
But I know you are
And so am I.

IV

Dale and I sojourned home
To spend
Long weekends
While you were
Able to enjoy
Our time together
We all grew closer
During those weekends
But they always
Ended
And I must admit
We were glad
To get in our car
And go back
To our simple lives
The stranger
Had decimated
Your body

That resembled
A Holocaust survivor
Only we all knew
You weren't
Going to be
A survivor
And it hurt
More than I can
Find words
To describe
To see you
That way
After the stranger
Had his way with you.

V

On weekend vigils
We sat waiting
Under the whirr
Of the ceiling fan
And amidst
Shrieks of joy
From grandchildren
Unaware
Of the presence
Of the stranger
Waiting
Just inside the door
Waiting

For the time, Ellen
When your spirit
Like the butterfly
Freeing itself
From its worldly cocoon
Takes flight
We sat waiting
Steeped in memories
Of days now faded
Into shadows
Of a happier past
Filled with love
And laughter
And promise.

Still we journeyed
To sit and wait
Watching for the stranger
While silently praying
For a miracle
Just one little miracle
To restore you to health.
Realistically praying
That the Father
Would take you home
Lifting you out
Of you pain racked body
Fervently praying
For the release
Of your spirit.

VI

Treatment day
Rolls round
Only this time
No talk
Of possibilities
Only nothingness
Three months
At the outside
You begin
To mark off
The days
On your calendar
As you race
Like a tortoise
To finish
The Pooh Bear rug
You are hooking
For your grandson
…still you remain
Cheerful
Even as you
Stare death in the face
You ask
If I will be all right
And through my tears
I lie.

VII

Dale, I watched you
Say goodbye
To our sister
Watched you
Who usually hug briefly
Complete with a back pat
Hold on to Ellen
To her life itself
Watched you hold on
As if for the last time
Embracing emaciated body
Shriveled skin hugging
Protruding bones
Stomach tumor swollen
Big enough to give life
Instead of take it.
Snapshot in my head
Clicking into memory
Randomly.

VIII

You chose
To take flight
While we were
On the highway
Somewhere
Between Atlanta

And Roanoke
We got to you
Before
Deaths angels came
To prepare you
For the tomb
And you were still propped up
On the sofa
With your hat
Hiding your bald head
And the sheet
Pulled up
To hide
You shriveled corpse
And we waited
For the death wagon
Knowing you had
Gone on
Your spirit
Fluttering
Away from us.
And we sighed
In relief.

IX

And now
Months later
I see you still
Sitting propped up

Hiding your bald head
Even in death
White cap
And white sheet
Your shroud
You're gone
Leaving us
Lonely for your smile.

Old Man, Where Have You Gone?

Old man
Where have you gone?
And why can't I hear your voice
Except in my head?

It hasn't been so long ago
That I stroked your fevered brow
To comfort you
While you lay limp
Hooked up to tubes and monitors.

It hasn't been so long ago
Since I sat on the floor
In the middle of the night
And listened to you snore
My knees drawn up
Under my chin
Eyes closed
Remembering days gone by
When I would lie in bed
Awakened by some demon

And took refuge in the safety
Of your snoring.

Old man
Where have you gone?
And why can't I hear your voice
Except in my head?

It hasn't been so long ago
When I stood and touched
Your cold brow
Looked at your marble face
Frozen in time.
Stood beside a solid, cherry coffin
Suffocating in the sickening sweet odor
Of funeral flowers.

And today
Some twenty years hence
I sit and weep
And wish I could touch
Your hands
That in their gentleness sustained me.

Old man
Where have you gone?
And why can't I hear your voice
Except in my head?

Waiting for Death

We wait
And she waits
As death reaches over her shoulder
To silently lay a hand on her
To hush the last gasp of air
Rattling in her cancer ridden lungs.

The funeral?
Yes, simple
Private graveside service
The dress to be her shroud
Yes, lovely. Already chosen
And we wait, stoically.

We wait
And she waits
As we compose her obituary
To note her accomplishments
Her contributions, her life
For the sorrow ridden community.

Her possessions?

Yes, decided
She has first choice
Her daughter, after all
Should have first choice
And we wait thoughtfully.

We watch
And she watches
As her body shrinks grotesquely
Shriveled skin hugging protruding bones
Festered lips housing muffled moans
To spare the sorrow ridden family.

Her pain?
Yes, demanding
I cannot bear her suffering
Her cross, after all
Is too heavy for me
And we wait rationally.

We wait
And she waits
As death, her soothing lover
Reaches silently to grasp her hand
And stealthily carry her shriveled remains
Away for our sorrow ridden eyes.

Our sorrow?
Yes, devastating
We cannot bear the void
Her absence leaves
Our lives painfully disrupted
And we sigh, thankfully.

The Remains of Life

Let us go and view the remains of life
Carried home form the hospital
And dumped on the kitchen floor
On the hard and cold kitchen floor
To be sorted out.

An empty suitcase gaping open
Like a mouth, gaping toothless, lifeless
The crumbled sleeping garments
Laying in a silken heap
Like a crouching corpse.

Let us go and view the remains of life
Dumped on the kitchen floor
The hard and cold kitchen floor.

Soiled garments dabbled with the colors
Of the rainbow, stretching over the heap
Empty bedroom slippers propped on the side
Of the empty suitcase, their golden color
Sparkling in a shaft of window light.

A make-up case filled with her secrets
Lipstick, power, perfume, all useless now
All occupying their own places
In her neatly stacked trays
Useful only to give her corpse the illusion of life.

Let us go and view the family
As their listless eyes stare blankly
At the remains of life scattered
On the hard and cold kitchen floor.

Swollen eyes, void of hope and illusion
Blankly stare at the lifeless heap…
As they try to grasp the finality of death
Figures frozen in time, stationary and silent
Struggling to sort out death's claim on life.

Let us go and view the remains of life
In a house with roaring silence and smell of death
That deadens the senses and leaves us
Numb, hopeless, shattered and afraid.

Among the last remains of life
Dumped on the kitchen floor
The hard and cold kitchen floor.
We sit afraid—afraid of the time
When our lives will be like this one
Scattered pell-mell upon a kitchen floor.

Vicky Lee, Feed My Birds and Squirrels

Mama
You came to see me today
As I filled the birdfeeders
In the back yard
I saw you in your baggy pants
And oversized shirt
Saw you open the back door
And toss out pieces of stale bread
To feed the birds and squirrels.

No fancy bird feeders
Or bird food
Too expensive to buy
No matter
You shared what you had
With birds and squirrels.

Death is not strong enough
To separate us.

And I realized
That I feed them
To honor you
And the kindness
To all living creatures
You taught me.

Death is not strong enough
To separate us.

So Mama
I celebrate you daily
In small ways
Natural gifts returned.

Daffodils and You

Daffodils herald spring's arrival
First spring you'll miss
I can close my eyes
And see you trapped in wheelchair
No you're screened in porch
Watching your friend
Spring arrive
Happy to be alive.

Daffodils
Jonquils
Yellow burst of sunlight
Break my heart
And make me smile
As I remember you.

"Vicky Lee,
Dig a big hole
Dump 50 bulbs in it,"
You said
And I did.
"They'll be sunshine
When they bloom,"
You said
And they are.

"Nickel dirt
And a $50 plant will die."
And it did.

You taught me to drink
The beauty
Of the daffodils in spring.
What you didn't teach me
Is how to look at the daffodils
And not cry for you.

Passing of a Generation

Dorothy died today at 94
What a void her death leaves
In our lives
So scattered far apart
Even though we no longer lived close
Or saw each other
Her persona was huge in my life
She was the last of the sisters
To go—the last born and the last to die.

I could not be there today at the viewing
Or tomorrow at the funeral
But I will celebrate her life anyway
I will remember the good times
Fun times
Picnics
Sunday afternoon ice cream rides
Hank Williams songs
The log cabin
Spend the nights at her house
Babysitting the girls.

I remember that she
Wanted her girls to be strong women
And named them after Deborah and Delilah in the Bible
I remember her driving without a driver's license
To take Mamaw to the doctor's office
Mostly I remember how much fun she was
I always had a good time with Aunt Dorothy.

Her passing marks the passing of a generation
Passing of all our mothers and fathers
All of the stories we never heard are gone
Family reunions are other worldly now.

So until we gather at the river
May they all watch over us.

Meanderings of a Poet

God
      Greatest poet of all
Set the world a-spinning
Raised her hands and said,
"Let there be light!"
Created woman and man
      Birds and animals
And it was good!

God makes thunder roar
Oceans swell
Holy spirit travel
Disguised as the wind.

The artist and poet
      Spew forth with
Pen and brush
      On paper and canvas yellowed
By time and the passing of youth.
      Long silent fingers splash hues
            Red,
Blue, green, yellow

Silhouettes her soul
And it is good.

Poet's hands conduct
   A symphony of sounds
That fall on ears
   At last open to hear
      The artist sees clearly
Yellowed canvas and poet's paper
   Resonate
      In hearts and souls
And it is good.

God, artist and poet
Trinity of wise women
Come bearing gifts
   Cascading
      One over the other
And it is GOOD!